NORTHERN HEMISPHERE

2023

FAMILY
ASTRONOMICAL
ALMANAC

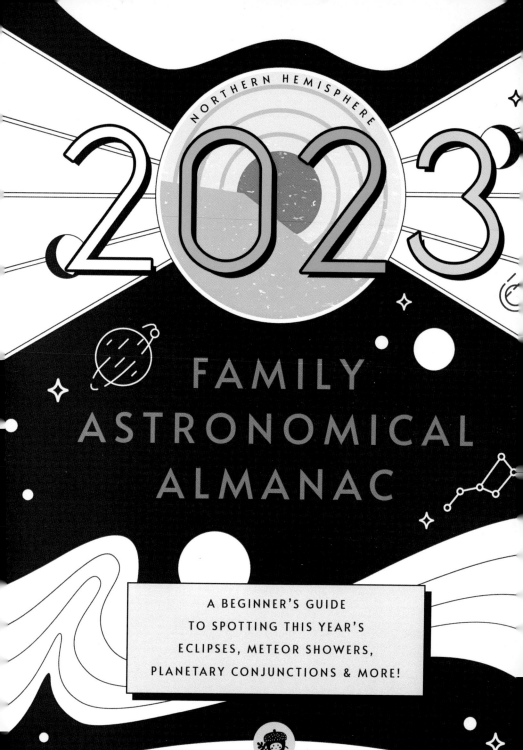

NORTHERN HEMISPHERE

2023

FAMILY ASTRONOMICAL ALMANAC

A BEGINNER'S GUIDE
TO SPOTTING THIS YEAR'S
ECLIPSES, METEOR SHOWERS,
PLANETARY CONJUNCTIONS & MORE!

INTRODUCTION

*W*elcome to the 2023 night sky! While many events are similar to those in 2022, there are some spectacular new ones this year (check out the annular eclipse on October 14 or the ever-rare blue moon on August 30!). As always, there's nothing quite so humbling and inspiring as spending an evening watching the dance of the heavens. It's even better when you do it with the people you love, which is why publishing this family guide to the events of the night sky is so exciting for us.

HOW WE CHOSE THE EVENTS

When it comes to astronomy, there is a lot to learn and a *lot* to observe! But in this book, we've picked out the most popular events that are easiest for beginner families and kids to tackle. You'll find eclipses, meteor showers, and planetary conjunctions, plus we've also noted some of the most significant orbital events of the year, like solstices and equinoxes.

DO I NEED A TELESCOPE?

If you have one, great! But if not, don't worry. We purposefully selected events that don't require any special equipment to see. In place of a telescope, you might consider binoculars, but even those are optional.

A NOTE ABOUT PHOTOGRAPHS

Wherever possible, we've included photographs of the actual astronomical events. In many cases, however, photos of comparable events or artistic renderings have had to be used instead. For planetary conjunctions, some photos feature conjunctions as they appear in the sky, while others show additional details of the planets up close.

With all that said, it's time to unfold some blankets, make a cup (or gallon) of cocoa, and get ready to wonder at the majesty of the heavens above. The night sky awaits!

Happy stargazing,

Bushel & Peck Books

HOW TO USE THIS BOOK

$\mathcal{E}$ach page of this book is designed to make it easy to find information about each astronomical event. Here's a quick tour:

DESCRIPTION: This will provide background information about the event, scientific explanations, and tips for getting the best views.

TYPE OF EVENT: In general, most events are categorized as planetary events, orbital milestones, eclipses, and meteor showers.

BEST VIEWING TIME: This recommends the best time of day to catch the event. If best viewing is advised for dusk, this means dusk of the date written. If best viewing is advised for dawn, this means the early morning of the date written. If viewing can occur all night, this means the evening of the date written, running into the early morning of the next day.

DIRECTION IN SKY: This advises the general area of the sky to look in. Please note that since the Earth is turning during the night, the exact location of stars and planets in the sky changes, too. Where you find the event in the sky might be different than what's written.

APR 23

CONJUNCTION OF MOON AND VENUS

Venus and the Moon will pass near each other in the night sky. Look high in the heavens in a western direction around dusk. The Moon will be easy to spot, of course; the bright spot nearby is Venus.

BEST VIEWING TIME: dusk until midnight

DIRECTION IN SKY: west

PLANETARY EVENT

CAN BE SEEN WITH NAKED EYE

40

EVENT NAME

APR 23

π-PUPPIDS METEOR SHOWER

Since it will occur close to a new Moon this year, the π-Puppid meteor shower will be particularly visible in the sky. For best viewing, look in a southwestern direction after dusk on the evening of April 23 (though the shower will happen between April 15 and April 28). The comet whose trail is responsible for the shower is 26P/Grigg-Skjellerup, which was first discovered in 1902. The comet was later visited in 1992 by the Giotto probe, an unmanned spacecraft from the European Space Agency.

METEOR SHOWER

RECURS ANNUALLY

CAN BE SEEN WITH NAKED EYE

....

BEST VIEWING TIME: just after dusk

....

PEAK: 10 meteors per hour

....

DIRECTION IN SKY: southwest (though meteors can radiate across most of the sky)

....

RADIANT: For meteor showers, we've included the radiant constellation. This is the point in the sky that the meteors will come from, and it's often what gives a meteor shower its name. But don't worry if these constellations are hard to spot in the sky—it's not necessary for enjoying the meteor shower, since meteors will radiate across most of the sky!

PEAK: This will tell you the highest level of activity a meteor shower is expected to reach (written in meteors per hour). However, remember that this is the projected number under ideal conditions like perfect darkness and clear skies. Chances are, the number of meteors you actually see will be much fewer (though still majestic!).

TIPS FOR STARGAZING

With a little preparation, you can make a night under the stars both fun and comfortable, not to mention memorable! Here are a few tips to do just that.

MAKE A PLAN. Pick where you're going to go (see below), know how long it will take to get there, and know when the event you want to observe is forecasted to occur. There's nothing more disappointing than doing all the work to catch a celestial event, only to be too late.

GO WHERE THERE IS AS LITTLE LIGHT AS POSSIBLE. Light pollution from cities and towns can make it much harder to see what's in the night sky. Find a place that is away from artificial light, like national and state parks, farms (with permission, of course), rural roads, and other places out in the country. It might mean a bit of a drive, but it will be worth it!

DRESS WARMLY. Even summer nights can get a little chilly sometimes. Dress in layers. On especially cold winter nights, you'll want hats, gloves, and even packaged hand warmers (they're wonderful!).

EXPECT SOME WAIT TIME. Waiting for a meteor shower to start or for an eclipse to begin requires some patience. This might be especially tough for younger kids, so plan ahead and bring snacks, games, and other fun activities to pass the time.

GET COMFORTABLE. Chairs, sleeping bags, pillows, and blankets can make the night hours nice and cozy. A little hot cocoa and some cookies don't hurt, either!

GLOSSARY

*T*hroughout this book, although we've tried to keep astronomical jargon to a minimum, you might find terms you're not familiar with. Here is a list of definitions to help.

asteroid: a body made from rock and metal that orbits the Sun

blue moon: the second full moon during the same calendar month

comet: a body made of rock and ice that orbits the Sun, usually with a tail of gas and debris

conjunction: when two bodies like the Moon or a planet appear especially near each other in the sky

constellation: a recognizable pattern or shape made from stars that goes by a universal name (e.g. the constellation Orion)

dawn: the twilight hours just before sunrise

dusk: the twilight hours just after sunset

full moon: the phase of the Moon when it is fully bright (see also "new moon" for comparison)

equinox: when the Sun is directly over the equator, resulting in equal day and night; this occurs two times per year (see Spring equinox on March 20 and September equinox on September 22)

gibbous: a word used to describe the Moon when it's more than half full; comes from *gibbus*, the Latin word for "humpback"

gravitational pull: the attractive force that one body exerts on another

horizon: where the sky and ground meet

lunar eclipse: when the shadow of the Earth falls on the Moon and reduces its light (see also "solar eclipse" for comparison)

meteor: a small piece of debris that burns when entering the Earth's atmosphere; also called a "shooting star"

meteor shower: a dense display of meteors, usually caused by the Earth moving through the debris trail of a comet or asteroid

meteorite: a meteor that doesn't completely burn up during its trip through the atmosphere and lands on the surface of the Earth

naked eye: with eyes only, without the aid of binoculars or telescopes

new moon: the phase of the Moon when it is completely dark (see also "full moon" for comparison)

orbit: the path a celestial body, like a planet or comet, takes around the Sun

peak: when the activity of a meteor shower is at its highest point (usually measured in meteors per hour)

radiant: the point in the sky from which a meteor shower issues (usually a constellation)

solar eclipse: when the Moon blocks the Sun and the Moon's shadow can be seen on Earth (see also "lunar eclipse" for comparison)

solstice: when the poles of the Earth are the closest or furthest away from the Sun (see "June solstice" on June 21 and "December solstice" on December 21)

waxing: when the amount of the Moon that is bright is increasing

waning: when the amount of the Moon that is bright is decreasing

Book Sources / Suggested Reading

- solarsystem.nasa.gov
- theskylive.com
- in-the-sky.org
- eclipse.gsfc.nasa.gov
- earthsky.org
- www.universeguide.com
- en.wikipedia.org
- www.space.com
- starwalk.space
- www.spacereference.org
- skyandtelescope.org
- sservi.nasa.gov
- www.mooninfo.org

CALENDAR

The following pages contain daily entries for each of the astronomical events scheduled to occur in 2023. Catch a meteor shower or spot a planet for the first time. The night sky is yours!

JAN 3

DID YOU KNOW? Mars is much smaller than Earth. If Earth were the size of a dime, Mars would only look like an aspirin tablet sitting next to it. But while Earth has only one moon, Mars has two!

PLANETARY
EVENT

CAN BE
SEEN WITH
NAKED EYE

CONJUNCTION OF MOON AND MARS

Mars and the Moon will be close together in the night sky. You can see them with the naked eye or with binoculars, but they might be too far apart to see through a telescope. Look for a bright point right near the Moon—that's Mars!

BEST VIEWING TIME: **dusk**

DIRECTION IN SKY: **south, moving to northwest**

PERIHELION

ORBITAL
MILESTONE

RECURS
ANNUALLY

The perihelion is the point in a planet's orbit when the planet is its closest to the Sun. Earth's perihelion occurs every year in January. You might wonder how Earth can be closer to the Sun at one time of the year and further away from it at another time. Doesn't it move in a circle? Not exactly. Earth's orbit is actually an ellipse, which means it moves in a slightly oval shape as it circles the Sun. As a result, it's a tiny bit closer to the Sun at some times, and a tiny bit farther away at other times.

Aphelion
July

Perihelion
January

152 million km   147 million km

RADIANT: Boötes

QUADRANTIDS METEOR SHOWER

METEOR SHOWER

RECURS ANNUALLY

CAN BE SEEN WITH NAKED EYE

One of the best meteor showers of the year, the Quadrantids meteor shower happens every January when the Earth passes through the orbit of an asteroid called 2003 EH1 (it's possible it might be a sort of dead comet, but scientists are still debating). The asteroid's trail is filled with debris—rocks, dust, bits of other asteroids—that burn up as they enter the Earth's atmosphere. The meteor shower usually lasts for a few hours, and then Earth must wait for another year to see it again.

BEST VIEWING TIME: during the night and predawn

PEAK: 60-200 meteors per hour!

DIRECTION IN SKY: north (though meteors can radiate across most of the sky)

JAN 19

γ-URSAE MINORIDS METEOR SHOWER

Though it occurs from around January 15 to January 22, the peak viewing time for the y-Ursae Minorids will be during the early morning of January 19. Look for the constellation Ursa Minor (the little bear, whose tail is Polaris, the North Star) and expect to see meteors radiating outwards from that area. This particular shower is not as intense as others, but there's still a good chance of seeing a shooting star.

METEOR SHOWER

RECURS ANNUALLY

CAN BE SEEN WITH NAKED EYE

BEST VIEWING TIME: during the night and predawn

PEAK: 3 meteors per hour

DIRECTION IN SKY: north (though meteors can radiate across most of the sky)

JAN 22

PLANETARY
EVENT

CAN BE
SEEN WITH
NAKED EYE

CONJUNCTION OF VENUS AND SATURN

Venus and Saturn will appear near each other at dusk. Look southwest for two bright points partway up above the horizon. Saturn has a much larger orbit than Venus (it's millions more miles away from the Sun), but the two do align in the night sky on a regular basis. Binoculars aren't required but will sure help!

BEST VIEWING TIME: **dusk**

DIRECTION IN SKY: **southwest**

CONJUNCTION OF MOON AND SATURN

Saturn and the Moon will be extremely close together in the night sky, making it easy to spot both at once. Binoculars might make it easier to see. Point them towards the Moon, which should be in a southwestern direction just above the horizon, and look for a bright point nearby.

PLANETARY EVENT

CAN BE SEEN WITH NAKED EYE

BEST VIEWING TIME: **dusk**

DIRECTION IN SKY: **southwest**

JAN 23

CONJUNCTION OF MOON AND VENUS

PLANETARY EVENT

CAN BE SEEN WITH NAKED EYE

Venus and the Moon will pass near each other in the night sky. Look high in the heavens in a southwestern direction around dusk. The Moon will be easy to spot, of course; the bright spot nearby is Venus.

BEST VIEWING TIME: **dusk**

DIRECTION IN SKY: **southwest**

JAN
25

CONJUNCTION OF MOON AND JUPITER

This will be a good chance to try to see Jupiter, since it will be near the Moon and the Moon will only be a few days old (so its light shouldn't overpower other points in the sky). Look for a bright point near the Moon around dusk!

PLANETARY EVENT

CAN BE SEEN WITH NAKED EYE

BEST VIEWING TIME: dusk

DIRECTION IN SKY: southwest

JAN 30

DID YOU KNOW? Mars gets its reddish color from iron minerals on the surface that rust and turn red.

PLANETARY EVENT

CAN BE SEEN WITH NAKED EYE

CONJUNCTION OF MOON AND MARS

Mars and the Moon will be extremely close together in the night sky, making it easy to spot both at once. You can see them with the naked eye or with binoculars, but they might be too far apart to see through a telescope. Look for a bright point right near the Moon—that's Mars!

BEST VIEWING TIME: **dusk and late evening**

DIRECTION IN SKY: **east, moving northwest**

FEB.
1

C/2022 E3 (ZTF) COMET AT ITS BRIGHTEST

This comet will be visible in the sky for several days, but experts project it will be at its brightest on February 1. Luckily, it's also expected to be in an area of night sky then that isn't especially full of stars. Find a patch of fairly blank sky just below the North Star. If you're lucky, the comet will be visible! (Even with an astronomer's best calculations, comet brightness is extremely difficult to predict, so this can be a tricky one to spot.)

COMET SIGHTING

BEST VIEWED WITH BINOCULARS

BEST VIEWING TIME: **all night**

DIRECTION IN SKY: **north**

FEB 15

CONJUNCTION OF VENUS AND NEPTUNE

PLANETARY
EVENT

CAN BE
SEEN WITH
NAKED EYE

Venus and Neptune will pass very near each other in the night sky, making them a little easier to pick out. When dusk falls, look in the western sky for two bright points next to each other.

BEST VIEWING TIME: **dusk**

DIRECTION IN SKY: **west**

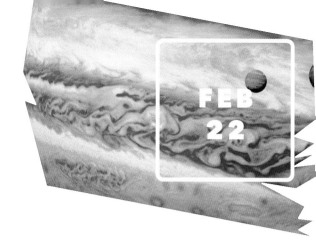

CONJUNCTION OF MOON AND JUPITER

Look for a bright point near the Moon above the western horizon, right around dusk. It will be visible for only a couple of hours after sunset.

BEST VIEWING TIME: **dusk**

DIRECTION IN SKY: **west**

PLANETARY EVENT

CAN BE SEEN WITH NAKED EYE

FEB 27

PLANETARY
EVENT

CAN BE
SEEN WITH
NAKED EYE

CONJUNCTION OF MOON AND MARS

Mars and the Moon will be extremely close together in the night sky. You can see them with the naked eye or with binoculars, but they might be too far apart to see through a telescope. Look for a reddish, bright point right near the Moon.

BEST VIEWING TIME: dusk to around midnight

DIRECTION IN SKY: southeast, moving northwest

CONJUNCTION OF VENUS AND JUPITER

Around dusk, look for two bright points a little above the horizon in the western sky. They will set below the horizon a couple of hours after sunset.

PLANETARY
EVENT

BEST VIEWING TIME: **dusk**

DIRECTION IN SKY: **west**

CAN BE
SEEN WITH
NAKED EYE

MAR 19

DID YOU KNOW? Saturn is considered a *gas giant*, which means it doesn't have a rocky surface like Earth but is instead made of swirling gas.

PLANETARY EVENT

CAN BE SEEN WITH NAKED EYE

CONJUNCTION OF MOON AND SATURN

Saturn and the Moon will be neighbors in the sky. Binoculars might make it easier to see. Point them towards the Moon, which should be in an eastern direction just barely above the horizon, and look for a bright point nearby.

BEST VIEWING TIME: **the hour before dawn**

DIRECTION IN SKY: **east**

MARCH EQUINOX

Also called the *spring equinox* or the *Vernal equinox*, the March equinox marks the point that the Sun aligns perfectly with the Earth's equator. Since the Earth is usually tilted towards or away from the Sun—the cause of the seasons—this perfect alignment during the equinox is unique. On this day, the Sun will rise from the exact east and set in the exact west. It will also produce almost exactly twelve hours of day and twelve hours of night in most parts of the world, which is where the term comes from: *aequus* (Latin for "equal") and *nox* (Latin for "night"). The March equinox marks the official beginning of spring.

ORBITAL
MILESTONE

RECURS
ANNUALLY

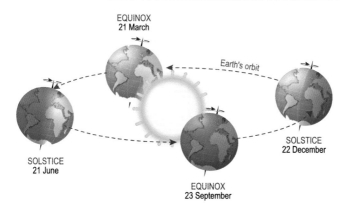

EQUINOX
21 March

Earth's orbit

SOLSTICE
21 June

SOLSTICE
22 December

EQUINOX
23 September

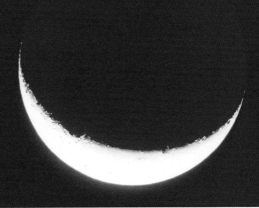

CONJUNCTION OF MOON AND JUPITER

PLANETARY
EVENT

CAN BE
SEEN WITH
NAKED EYE

This is another chance to catch Jupiter passing nearby the Moon! Look for a bright point near the Moon, just above the western horizon during dusk.

BEST VIEWING TIME: dusk

DIRECTION IN SKY: west

DID YOU KNOW? Mars is named for the Roman god of war. It's reddish color reminded people of blood!

CONJUNCTION OF MOON AND MARS

You can see both Mars and the Moon when they're extremely close together in the night sky on March 28. Look for a bright point right near the Moon—that's Mars!

PLANETARY EVENT

CAN BE SEEN WITH NAKED EYE

BEST VIEWING TIME: late evening to midnight

DIRECTION IN SKY: southwest

APR 15

CONJUNCTION OF MOON AND SATURN

PLANETARY EVENT

CAN BE SEEN WITH NAKED EYE

Saturn and the Moon will be extremely close together in the night sky, making it easy to spot both at once. Binoculars might make Saturn easier to see. Look in a southeastern direction just above the horizon.

BEST VIEWING TIME: **the two hours before dawn**

DIRECTION IN SKY: **southeast**

LYRIDS METEOR SHOWER

Less active than the Quadrantids but more so than the γ-Ursae Minorids, the Lyrid meteor shower produces a peak of seventeen meteors per hour. This will be easiest to observe during the early morning hours before dawn on April 22, though the shower will still be happening (with less intensity) between April 16 and April 25. The comet C/1861 G1 is responsible for the Lyrid meteor shower, its trail of rocky particles burning up in the Earth's atmosphere as the Earth passes through.

METEOR SHOWER

RECURS ANNUALLY

CAN BE SEEN WITH NAKED EYE

BEST VIEWING TIME: late evening to the hours just before dawn

PEAK: 17 meteors per hour

DIRECTION IN SKY: north-northeast (though meteors can radiate across most of the sky)

APR 23

CONJUNCTION OF MOON AND VENUS

PLANETARY
EVENT

CAN BE
SEEN WITH
NAKED EYE

Venus and the Moon will pass near each other in the night sky. Look high in the heavens in a western direction around dusk. The Moon will be easy to spot, of course; the bright spot nearby is Venus.

BEST VIEWING TIME: **dusk until midnight**

DIRECTION IN SKY: **west**

APR 23

π-PUPPIDS METEOR SHOWER

Since it will occur close to a new Moon this year, the π-Puppid meteor shower will be particularly visible in the sky. For best viewing, look in a southwestern direction after dusk on the evening of April 23 (though the shower will happen between April 15 and April 28). The comet whose trail is responsible for the shower is 26P/Grigg-Skjellerup, which was first discovered in 1902. The comet was later visited in 1992 by the Giotto probe, an unmanned spacecraft from the European Space Agency.

METEOR SHOWER

RECURS ANNUALLY

CAN BE SEEN WITH NAKED EYE

BEST VIEWING TIME: just after dusk

PEAK: 10 meteors per hour

DIRECTION IN SKY: southwest (though meteors can radiate across most of the sky)

APR 25

DID YOU KNOW? Billions of years ago, Mars was likely a warm planet that even had oceans and rain!

PLANETARY EVENT

CAN BE SEEN WITH NAKED EYE

CONJUNCTION OF MOON AND MARS

You can see them with the naked eye or with binoculars, but they might be too far apart to see through a telescope. Look for a bright point right near the Moon—that's Mars!

BEST VIEWING TIME: **dusk**

DIRECTION IN SKY: **west**

η-AQUARIIDS METEOR SHOWER

The η-Aquariid meteor shower happens every year when the Earth passes through the trail of none other than Halley's Comet, arguably the most famous comet in space. The peak of the meteor shower will occur around May 6 and will be most visible between the hours of 3:00 am and 5:30 am in a southeastern direction. Halley's Comet visits the Earth roughly every seventy-five years, and stargazers first noticed it as early as 240 BC (though it wasn't until 1705 that Edmond Halley realized it was a recurring visitor).

METEOR SHOWER

RECURS ANNUALLY

CAN BE SEEN WITH NAKED EYE

BEST VIEWING TIME: between 3:00 am and 5:30 am

PEAK: 40 meteors per hour

DIRECTION IN SKY: southeast (though meteors can radiate across most of the sky)

RADIANT: Lyra

η-LYRIDS METEOR SHOWER

One of the quieter meteor showers, the η-Lyrid meteor shower happens when the Earth passes through the trail of comet C/1983 H1. The shower will be visible all night, with peak visibility happening around 5:00 am.

METEOR SHOWER

RECURS ANNUALLY

CAN BE SEEN WITH NAKED EYE

BEST VIEWING TIME: early hours just before dawn

PEAK: 3 meteors per hour

DIRECTION IN SKY: northeast (though meteors can radiate across most of the sky)

DID YOU KNOW? Saturn's density is actually less than that of water. If there were a bathtub the size of the solar system filled with water, Saturn would float!

CONJUNCTION OF MOON AND SATURN

Saturn and the Moon will be extremely close together in the night sky. Look towards the Moon, which should be in a southern direction just above the horizon, and search for a bright point nearby.

BEST VIEWING TIME: **the two hours before dawn**

DIRECTION IN SKY: **southeast**

PLANETARY
EVENT

CAN BE
SEEN WITH
NAKED EYE

MAY 17

DID YOU KNOW? The red spot on Jupiter is actually a gigantic, swirling storm with winds as high as 400 miles per hour (a Category 5 hurricane needs winds of only 158 miles per hour).

CONJUNCTION OF MOON AND JUPITER

PLANETARY EVENT

Look for a bright point near the Moon above the southeastern horizon just before dawn.

....

BEST VIEWING TIME: the two hours before dawn

....

DIRECTION IN SKY: *east*

....

CAN BE SEEN WITH NAKED EYE

DID YOU KNOW? It takes light from Sun almost fourteen minutes to finally reach Mars.

CONJUNCTION OF MOON AND MARS

Look for a bright point right near the Moon—that's Mars!

BEST VIEWING TIME: **dusk**

DIRECTION IN SKY: **west**

PLANETARY EVENT

CAN BE SEEN WITH NAKED EYE

CONJUNCTION OF MOON AND SATURN

PLANETARY
EVENT

CAN BE
SEEN WITH
NAKED EYE

Saturn and the Moon will once again be extremely close together in the night sky. Binoculars might make Saturn easier to see. Point them towards the Moon, which should be in a southern direction just above the horizon, and look for a bright point nearby.

....

BEST VIEWING TIME: **midnight until dawn**

....

DIRECTION IN SKY: **south**

....

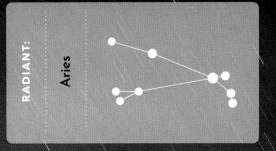

RADIANT: Aries

 ARIETIDS METEOR SHOWER

The Arietids meteor shower has one of the higher meteor frequency rates, averaging over fifty meteors per hour at its peak. The shower is active from April 14 until June 24, but the most intense meteor activity is expected near dawn on June 11. Scientists don't yet know the source of the Arietids.

METEOR SHOWER

....

BEST VIEWING TIME: the two hours before dawn

....

RECURS ANNUALLY

PEAK: 50-60 meteors per hour

....

DIRECTION IN SKY: north (though meteors can radiate across most of the sky)

....

CAN BE SEEN WITH NAKED EYE

JUNE SOLSTICE

This marks the first day of summer in the Northern Hemisphere (hence it is sometimes called the summer solstice). It occurs when the northern pole of the Earth is pointed most directly at the Sun. As a result, it is also the longest day of the year, with cities in the extreme north experiencing daylight nearly all day long—twenty-two hours of light in Fairbanks, Alaska, and a full twenty-four hours in Mumansk, Russia—and cities further south still having longer-than-usual light—sixteen hours in Paris, and fifteen hours in New York. So get up early and play long into the night; you'll have plenty of light!

ORBITAL
MILESTONE

RECURS
ANNUALLY

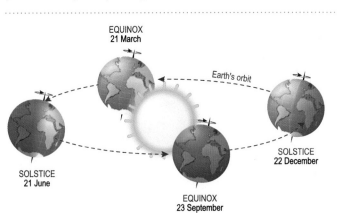

EQUINOX
21 March

Earth's orbit

SOLSTICE
22 December

SOLSTICE
21 June

EQUINOX
23 September

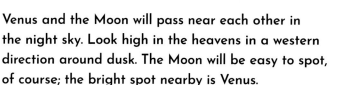

CONJUNCTION OF MOON AND VENUS

Venus and the Moon will pass near each other in the night sky. Look high in the heavens in a western direction around dusk. The Moon will be easy to spot, of course; the bright spot nearby is Venus.

BEST VIEWING TIME: **dusk**

DIRECTION IN SKY: **west**

PLANETARY
EVENT

CAN BE
SEEN WITH
NAKED EYE

JUN 22

DID YOU KNOW? It takes Mars almost twice as long as the Earth to complete an orbit around the Sun.

PLANETARY EVENT

CAN BE SEEN WITH NAKED EYE

CONJUNCTION OF MOON, VENUS, AND MARS

You'll have a chance to catch all three of these together in the sky on the night of June 22. Look above the western horizon right around dusk. Hurry though—they'll set just a couple of hours after the sun does!

BEST VIEWING TIME: **dusk**

DIRECTION IN SKY: **west**

BOOTIDS METEOR SHOWER

As the Earth passes through the trail of comet 7P/ Pons-Winnecke, expect to see the Bootid meteor shower between June 22 and July 2. The peak will occur on June 27, with the best time to view soon after nightfall (though the shower will be visible above the horizon all night). Comet Pons-Winnecke was discovered in 1819. Scientists estimate that its head is over three miles wide! Though there are usually only one or two meteors per hour even at the shower's peak, the Bootid shower is known for producing slower moving meteors than other showers.

BEST VIEWING TIME: right after dusk

PEAK: 1-2 meteors per hour

DIRECTION IN SKY: northeast (though meteors can radiate across most of the sky)

METEOR SHOWER

RECURS ANNUALLY

CAN BE SEEN WITH NAKED EYE

APHELION

ORBITAL
MILESTONE

RECURS
ANNUALLY

The aphelion is the point in a planet's orbit when the planet is furthest from the Sun. Earth's aphelion occurs every year in July, whereas its perihelion—the point it's *closest* to the Sun—occurs in January (see "Perihelion" on January 4). During the aphelion, the Sun will technically appear smaller in the sky than on any other day. However, since it's only about 3 percent smaller than usual, it's unlikely you'll notice!

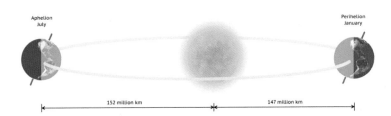

Aphelion
July

Perihelion
January

152 million km   147 million km

DID YOU KNOW? Saturn isn't the only planet with rings. Jupiter, Neptune, and Uranus (depicted here)each have rings as well, though theirs are much more faint.

CONJUNCTION OF MOON AND SATURN

Look towards the Moon, which should be in an eastern direction above the horizon, and search for a bright point nearby.

PLANETARY EVENT

BEST VIEWING TIME: **between midnight and dawn**

DIRECTION IN SKY: **east, moving south**

CAN BE SEEN WITH NAKED EYE

PLANETARY
EVENT

CAN BE
SEEN WITH
NAKED EYE

VENUS AT ITS BRIGHTEST

Named after the Roman God of love, Venus is the second planet from the sun and one of Earth's neighbors. This will be one of the best times of the year to see the planet Venus. Why? Because Venus, which is usually close to the sun in the sky, will finally be further away in its orbit, allowing its own light to really shine. In fact, Venus will be the third-brightest object in the sky on this night (behind only the moon and sun themselves)!

BEST VIEWING TIME: **dusk**

DIRECTION IN SKY: **west**

JUL 11

CONJUNCTION OF MOON AND JUPITER

Look for a bright point near the Moon above the eastern horizon in the hours before or near dawn.

BEST VIEWING TIME: **before and around dawn**

DIRECTION IN SKY: **east**

PLANETARY EVENT

CAN BE SEEN WITH NAKED EYE

JUL
20

DID YOU KNOW? Venus, Earth, and Mars are all neighbors, and yet the temperature on Venus's surface is hot enough to melt lead, while the surface on Mars is so cold that water instantly freezes. Earth is a pretty good place to call home!

PLANETARY
EVENT

CAN BE
SEEN WITH
NAKED EYE

CONJUNCTION OF MOON, VENUS, AND MARS

Mars, Venus, and the Moon will all appear near each other in the evening sky. Look for the Moon, then locate two bright points nearby. Fortunately, the Moon will be only a few days old, so its light shouldn't overpower the planets nearby.

BEST VIEWING TIME: **dusk**

DIRECTION IN SKY: **west**

CONJUNCTION OF VENUS AND MERCURY

Venus and Mercury will pass very near each other, making them a little easier to pick out. However, they'll mostly be in the sky during the daytime, so the only chance to see them is right at dusk when, for a few minutes, they'll be just above the horizon.

PLANETARY EVENT

CAN BE SEEN WITH NAKED EYE

....

BEST VIEWING TIME: **dusk**

....

DIRECTION IN SKY: **south**

....

JUL 29

PISCIS AUSTRINIDS METEOR SHOWER

METEOR SHOWER

RECURS ANNUALLY

CAN BE SEEN WITH NAKED EYE

Occurring between July 15 through August 10 but with a peak on July 29, the Piscis Austrinids happen when the Earth passes through a space trail of debris left from an unknown object (some scientists think it may be a comet or asteroid that has since disintegrated). This particular shower is usually somewhat faint, so viewing is best during the darkest hours of the night. Unfortunately, the Moon will be bright this year, so meteors might be especially hard to spot.

BEST VIEWING TIME: **after midnight**

PEAK: **5 meteors per hour**

DIRECTION IN SKY: **south (though meteors can radiate across most of the sky)**

**JUL
30**

SOUTHERN
δ-AQUARIIDS
METEOR SHOWER

The Southern δ-Aquariids (not to be confused with the η-Aquariids on May 6) occur around the same time as the Piscis Austrinids and are usually a little easier to see. Producing around twenty-five meteors per hour at its peak, the Aquariids happen between July 12 and August 23 with a peak on July 30. The shower begins when the Earth enters the orbit of comet P/2008 Y12 (SOHO). SOHO takes over five years to complete an orbit around the Sun, and though its orbit takes it very close to the Earth, scientists say that simulations don't forecast a future collision. Whew!

METEOR
SHOWER

RECURS
ANNUALLY

CAN BE
SEEN WITH
NAKED EYE

BEST VIEWING TIME: between midnight and sunrise

PEAK: 25 meteors per hour

DIRECTION IN SKY: east (though meteors can radiate across most of the sky)

α-CAPRICORNIDS METEOR SHOWER

Active from July 3 until August 15 but with a peak on July 30, the Capricornids radiate from a point near—you guessed it—the Capricornus constellation. At its peak, the shower produces around only five meteors per hour, but since Capricornus will be above the horizon most of the night, the shower can be viewed during all nighttime hours. The best viewing will be in a southern direction shortly after midnight. The comet trail responsible for the meteor shower belongs to comet 169P/NEAT, which scientists believe might have broken off from the same celestial body as P/2008 T12 (SOHO) nearly 3,000 years ago.

METEOR SHOWER

RECURS ANNUALLY

CAN BE SEEN WITH NAKED EYE

BEST VIEWING TIME: just after midnight, though visible all night

PEAK: 5 meteors per hour

DIRECTION IN SKY: east (though meteors can radiate across most of the sky)

DID YOU KNOW?
Each of Saturn's rings orbits the planet at a different speed.

CONJUNCTION OF MOON AND SATURN

Saturn and the Moon will again be near each other in the night sky. Look towards the Moon, which should be in an eastern direction above the horizon, and then look for a bright point nearby.

PLANETARY EVENT

CAN BE SEEN WITH NAKED EYE

BEST VIEWING TIME: **after dusk but before midnight**

DIRECTION IN SKY: **east, moving southwest**

AUG 8

DID YOU KNOW? Jupiter's largest moons were discovered by Galileo in 1610. One is as large as Mercury, and another may have underground oceans!

CONJUNCTION OF MOON AND JUPITER

This is another chance to catch Jupiter passing nearby the Moon. Look for a bright point near the Moon above the southeastern horizon around dawn.

PLANETARY EVENT

BEST VIEWING TIME: **dawn**

DIRECTION IN SKY: **southeast**

CAN BE SEEN WITH NAKED EYE

RADIANT: Perseus

AUG 13

✵ PERSEIDS METEOR SHOWER

Like the Quadrantids, the Perseids shower is one of the best meteor showers of the year, producing around 150 meteors per hour during its peak. The shower occurs between July 17 and August 24, with the highest rate of meteors happening during the early morning of August 13. Fortunately, this year the Moon will be nearly dark at that time, so the Perseids could be especially visible. The Perseids occur when the Earth passes through the orbit of comet 109P/Swift-Tuttle, which was first discovered in 1862. It's a massive comet with a head nearly sixteen miles across!

METEOR SHOWER

RECURS ANNUALLY

CAN BE SEEN WITH NAKED EYE

BEST VIEWING TIME: just before dawn, though visible all night

PEAK: 150 meteors per hour!

DIRECTION IN SKY: northeast (though meteors can radiate across most of the sky)

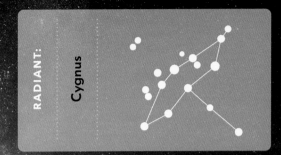

AUG 18

κ-CYGNIDS METEOR SHOWER

METEOR SHOWER

RECURS ANNUALLY

CAN BE SEEN WITH NAKED EYE

Though among the less dramatic meteor showers, the Cygnids are a last chance to catch some shooting stars during the warm summer. The shower occurs between August 3 and August 25. Its peak, on August 18, can produce around five meteors per hour. Because of its close timing to the Perseids, early observers didn't realize it was a separate meteor shower until 1877.

....

BEST VIEWING TIME: before midnight, though visible all night

....

PEAK: 5 meteors per hour

....

DIRECTION IN SKY: north-northwest (though meteors can radiate across most of the sky)

....

BLUE MOON

A "Blue Moon" is when there are two full Moons in the same month. The Blue Moon is the second full Moon (and no, it's not really blue). Blue Moons only happen about once every three years, so now you also know why people say "once in a Blue Moon" to describe something rare! This year, the Moon will look especially large because of its close proximity to the Earth.

BLUE MOON

CAN BE SEEN WITH NAKED EYE

BEST VIEWING TIME: **just before dawn**

DIRECTION IN SKY: **southeast**

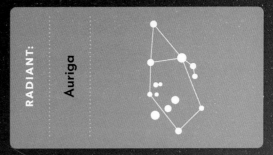

RADIANT: Auriga

AURIGIDS METEOR SHOWER

METEOR
SHOWER

RECURS
ANNUALLY

CAN BE
SEEN WITH
NAKED EYE

At their height, the Aurigids produce around six meteors per hour, with a peak occurring on September 1 (though the shower happens between August 28 and September 5). The meteor shower begins when the Earth moves through the orbit of comet C/1911 N1 (Kiess), which was first discovered in 1911. Visibility will be a little more challenging this year because of the shower occuring so close to a full Moon.

BEST VIEWING TIME: **just before dawn**

PEAK: **6 meteors per hour**

DIRECTION IN SKY: **east-northeast (though meteors can radiate across most of the sky)**

CONJUNCTION OF MOON AND JUPITER

This is another chance to catch Jupiter passing nearby the Moon. Look for a bright point near the Moon between midnight and dawn.

PLANETARY EVENT

CAN BE SEEN WITH NAKED EYE

BEST VIEWING TIME: **between midnight and dawn**

DIRECTION IN SKY: **east, moving southwest**

SEP 16

DID YOU KNOW? People have studied Mars as far back as the Egyptians, who tracked its movements in the sky 4,000 years ago.

PLANETARY
EVENT

CAN BE
SEEN WITH
NAKED EYE

CONJUNCTION OF MOON AND MARS

If you can catch them right before they slip under the horizon at dusk, look for a bright point right near the Moon. That's Mars!

BEST VIEWING TIME: **right at dusk**

DIRECTION IN SKY: **southeast**

VENUS AT ITS BRIGHTEST

For the second time, this will be one of the best times of the year to see the planet Venus since it will be at its brightest. The best time to spot it is just before sunrise. Look towards the east, a little above the horizon.

PLANETARY EVENT

CAN BE SEEN WITH NAKED EYE

BEST VIEWING TIME: **just before dawn**

DIRECTION IN SKY: **east**

SEPTEMBER EQUINOX

Like its counterpart, the March equinox (see March 20), the September equinox marks the point that the Sun again aligns perfectly with the Earth's equator. As you'll recall, since the Earth is usually tilted towards or away from the Sun—the cause of the seasons—this perfect alignment during the equinox is unique. On this day, the Sun will rise from the exact east and set in the exact west. It will also produce almost exactly twelve hours of day and twelve hours of night in most parts of the world. The September equinox signals the beginning of the fall season.

ORBITAL
MILESTONE

RECURS
ANNUALLY

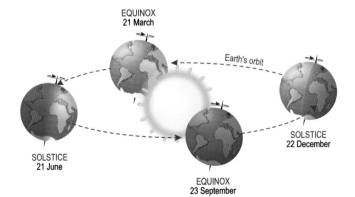

EQUINOX
21 March

Earth's orbit

SOLSTICE
21 June

SOLSTICE
22 December

EQUINOX
23 September

DID YOU KNOW? Saturn's rings were named alphabetically (Ring A, Ring B, and so on) in the order they were discovered, not the order in which they surround the planet.

CONJUNCTION OF MOON AND SATURN

Saturn and the Moon will be close together in the night sky. Binoculars might make it easier to see. Point them towards the Moon, which should be in a southern direction above the horizon, and look for a bright point nearby.

PLANETARY EVENT

CAN BE SEEN WITH NAKED EYE

BEST VIEWING TIME: **between dusk and midnight**

DIRECTION IN SKY: **south**

SEP 28

SEXTANTIDS METEOR SHOWER

METEOR SHOWER

RECURS ANNUALLY

CAN BE SEEN WITH NAKED EYE

Occurring between September 9 and October 9, the Sextantids peak on September 27 with a climax of between five to twenty meteors per hour. Unlike other meteor showers, the source of the Sextantids is not a comet but an asteroid: asteroid 2005 UD, to be precise. Scientists believe that asteroid 2005 UD might be another break-off from a larger body. As the Earth passes through asteroid 2005 UD's trail, bits of debris burn up in our atmosphere and become shooting stars.

BEST VIEWING TIME: **early morning before dawn**

PEAK: **5-20 meteors per hour**

DIRECTION IN SKY: **east (though meteors can radiate across most of the sky)**

DID YOU KNOW? Jupiter is made of all the same gases and materials as a star, but scientists believe it simply wasn't large or hot enough to ignite into one.

CONJUNCTION OF MOON AND JUPITER

Look for a bright point near the Moon above the eastern horizon but moving steadily westward.

PLANETARY EVENT

BEST VIEWING TIME: **before dawn**

DIRECTION IN SKY: **east, moving west**

CAN BE SEEN WITH NAKED EYE

OCT 6

METEOR SHOWER

RECURS ANNUALLY

CAN BE SEEN WITH NAKED EYE

CAMELOPARDALIDS METEOR SHOWER

The Camelopardalids occur when the Earth passes through the tail of comet 209P/LINEAR (once thought to be an asteroid). It's among the quietest showers of the year, with only around two meteors per hour even at its peak. The best time to view the shower is just before dawn near the North Star.

BEST VIEWING TIME: early morning before dawn

PEAK: 2 meteors per hour

DIRECTION IN SKY: north (though meteors can radiate across most of the sky)

OCT 9

DRACONIDS METEOR SHOWER

Though typically a quieter meteor shower with around ten to twenty meteors per hour, the Draconids can sometimes be quite dramatic: observers in Europe counted over 600 meteors per hour in 2011! The source of the Draconids is the comet 21P/Giacobini-Zinner, which left a particularly condensed trail of dust and debris when it passed through the area in 1900.

METEOR SHOWER

RECURS ANNUALLY

CAN BE SEEN WITH NAKED EYE

BEST VIEWING TIME: just after dusk or right before dawn

PEAK: 10-20 meteors per hour

DIRECTION IN SKY: northwest (though meteors can radiate across most of the sky)

OCT 10

CONJUNCTION OF MOON AND VENUS

PLANETARY
EVENT

CAN BE
SEEN WITH
NAKED EYE

Venus and the Moon will pass near each other in the night sky. Look high in the heavens in an eastern direction in the early hours just before dawn. The Moon will be easy to spot, of course; the bright spot nearby is Venus.

BEST VIEWING TIME: **the two hours before dawn**

DIRECTION IN SKY: **east**

OCT 10

SOUTHERN TAURIDS METEOR SHOWER

Though producing around only five meteors per hour, the Southern Taurids are a surprisingly steady meteor shower between September 10 and November 20 (yes, that long!) that produces a fair number of fireballs. October 10 is expected to be the shower's peak, and fortunately, the Moon will be a small crescent on that day and less likely to obscure the meteor shower.

BEST VIEWING TIME: **early morning before dawn**

PEAK: **5 meteors per hour**

DIRECTION IN SKY: **northeast (though meteors can radiate across most of the sky)**

METEOR SHOWER

RECURS ANNUALLY

CAN BE SEEN WITH NAKED EYE

⊛ ANNULAR SOLAR ECLIPSE

SOLAR
ECLIPSE

AVOID
LOOKING
DIRECTLY AT
THE SUN

This eclipse will be one of the highlights of the year! Annular solar eclipses happen when the Moon moves in front of the Sun without fully blocking it, creating a halo of light around a darkened center. The eclipse will be at least partially visible across all of North America, with the most pronounced effect happening in a corridor across the southwest U.S. between California and Texas.

BEST VIEWING TIME: **varies by location**

DIRECTION IN SKY: **varies by location**

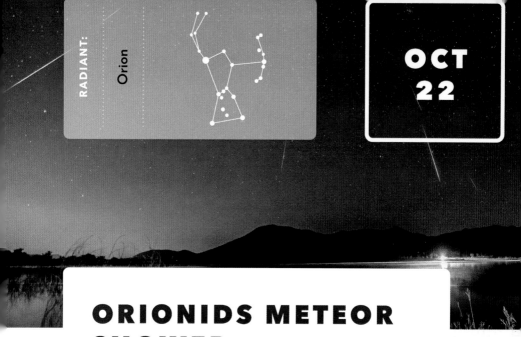

RADIANT: Orion

OCT 22

ORIONIDS METEOR SHOWER

Another meteor shower caused by Comet Halley (see the η-Aquariid meteor shower on May 6), the Orionids shower is a reliable fall favorite. The peak will happen around October 21 with roughly fifteen meteors per hour. The best viewing time is just before dawn. Meteors will radiate from around the Orion constellation (recognizable from the belt made of three stars close in a row).

METEOR SHOWER

RECURS ANNUALLY

CAN BE SEEN WITH NAKED EYE

BEST VIEWING TIME: just before dawn

PEAK: 15 meteors per hour

DIRECTION IN SKY: northeast (though meteors can radiate across most of the sky)

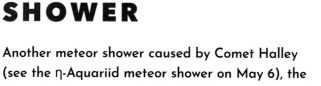

OCT 24

CONJUNCTION OF MOON AND SATURN

PLANETARY EVENT

CAN BE SEEN WITH NAKED EYE

Saturn and the Moon will be near one another in the night sky. Look for a bright point near the Moon in a southern direction during the late evening.

BEST VIEWING TIME: late evening to around midnight

DIRECTION IN SKY: southeast moving southwest

DID YOU KNOW?
Jupiter is twice as big
as *all* the other planets
put together!

CONJUNCTION OF MOON AND JUPITER

Jupiter and the Moon will be extremely close together in the night sky, making it easy to spot both at once. You can see them with the naked eye or with binoculars, but they might be too far apart to see through a telescope. Look for a bright point right near the Moon—that's Jupiter!

PLANETARY EVENT

CAN BE SEEN WITH NAKED EYE

BEST VIEWING TIME: **before dawn**

DIRECTION IN SKY: **east, moving west**

NOV 9

PLANETARY
EVENT

CAN BE
SEEN WITH
NAKED EYE

CONJUNCTION OF MOON AND VENUS

Venus and the Moon will pass near each other in the night sky. Look high in the heavens in a southern direction in the early hours just before dawn. The Moon will be easy to spot, of course; the bright spot nearby is Venus.

BEST VIEWING TIME: **the two hours before dawn**

DIRECTION IN SKY: **south**

NORTHERN TAURIDS METEOR SHOWER

Cousin of the Southern Taurids (see October 10), the Northern Taurids are caused by the same comet (comet 2P/Encke). Scientists believe that Jupiter's gravitational pull may have warped the comet's trail into two streams. Hence, there is a Northern and Southern variety, with both showers overlapping and adding to the overall volume of meteors. The Taurids are known for producing particularly bright meteors, which some observers have dubbed "Halloween fireballs."

METEOR SHOWER

RECURS ANNUALLY

CAN BE SEEN WITH NAKED EYE

BEST VIEWING TIME: midnight

PEAK: 5 meteors per hour

DIRECTION IN SKY: northeast (though meteors can radiate across most of the sky)

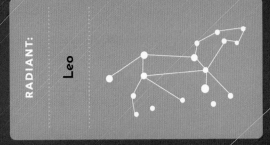

RADIANT: Leo

LEONIDS METEOR SHOWER

METEOR SHOWER

RECURS ANNUALLY

CAN BE SEEN WITH NAKED EYE

The Leonids are active from November 6 through November 30, but the peak will occur on November 18 when scientists predict around 15-20 meteors per hour. The comet Tempel-Tuttle is responsible for the shower, and it occasionally produces meteor storms with thousands of meteors every hour (though this isn't predicted for this year).

BEST VIEWING TIME: **just before dawn**

PEAK: **15 meteors per hour**

DIRECTION IN SKY: **east (though meteors can radiate across most of the sky)**

NOV 22

α-MONOCEROTIDS METEOR SHOWER

The Monocerotids meteor shower produces a modest volume of meteors, but it can vary widely year over year. Outbursts with hundreds or thousands of meteors every hour were observed in 1925, 1935, 1985, and 1995, and having one again depends on conditions being just right (it was predicted for 2019 but didn't come to pass). No such outburst is expected this year, but as with all meteor showers, the Monocerotids are unpredictable. It's little wonder that some stargazers call them "unicorn meteors," and not just because they radiate near Monoceros, the unicorn constellation!

METEOR SHOWER

RECURS ANNUALLY

CAN BE SEEN WITH NAKED EYE

BEST VIEWING TIME: **between midnight and dawn**

PEAK: **varies**

DIRECTION IN SKY: **east (though meteors can radiate across most of the sky)**

RADIANT: Hydra

σ-HYDRIDS
METEOR SHOWER

METEOR
SHOWER

RECURS
ANNUALLY

CAN BE
SEEN WITH
NAKED EYE

The Sigma Hydrids are slower in general, with around three meteors per hour at the shower's peak, but they're known for producing brighter-than-average meteors. They occur from December 3 through December 15, with the peak happening around December 12. For best viewing, watch the night sky between midnight and dawn in a northwestern direction (though, as with all meteor showers, meteors can radiate across most of the sky, so don't be too stressed about looking in the right direction).

BEST VIEWING TIME: **between midnight and dawn**

PEAK: **3 meteors per hour**

DIRECTION IN SKY: **northwestern (though meteors can radiate across most of the sky)**

RADIANT: Gemini

DEC 14

⊛ GEMINIDS METEOR SHOWER

One of the best (and most reliable) meteor showers of the year, the Geminids take place between December 4 and December 17, with the peak occurring during the early morning of December 14 around 2 am. Forecasts predict as many as 120 meteors per hour during the peak, so this is one to watch. The Geminids occur when the Earth passes through the orbit of asteroid 3200 Phaethon (though some call it a "rock comet"), which was first discovered in 1983 when scientists were reviewing images taken by a satellite.

METEOR SHOWER

RECURS ANNUALLY

CAN BE SEEN WITH NAKED EYE

BEST VIEWING TIME: **between midnight and dawn (2 am is best)**

PEAK: **120 meteors per hour**

DIRECTION IN SKY: **east (though meteors can radiate across most of the sky)**

DEC 16

COMAE BERENICIDS METEOR SHOWER

Though it's one of the harder meteor showers to see—and one of the least active—it's worth mentioning the Comae Berenicids because they produce some of the fastest meteors in the night sky. Occurring between December 12 and December 23, the Comae Berenicids peak on December 16 with a zenith of around three meteors per hour.

METEOR SHOWER

RECURS ANNUALLY

CAN BE SEEN WITH NAKED EYE

BEST VIEWING TIME: just before dawn

PEAK: 3 meteors per hour

DIRECTION IN SKY: northwest (though meteors can radiate across most of the sky)

DEC 20

DECEMBER LEONIS MINORIDS METEOR SHOWER

Not to be confused with the regular Leonis Minorids (see November 18), the December Leonis Minorids can produce up to five meteors per hour at its peak, which occurs on December 20. The shower itself lasts from December 5 until February 4.

....

BEST VIEWING TIME: between midnight and dawn

....

PEAK: 5 meteors per hour

....

DIRECTION IN SKY: northwest (though meteors can radiate across most of the sky)

....

METEOR SHOWER

RECURS ANNUALLY

CAN BE SEEN WITH NAKED EYE

DEC 21

DECEMBER SOLSTICE

ORBITAL
MILESTONE

RECURS
ANNUALLY

This marks the first day of winter in the Northern Hemisphere (hence it is sometimes called the winter solstice). It occurs when the northern pole of the Earth is pointed its furthest from the Sun. As a result, it is also the shortest day of the year, with cities in the extreme north experiencing darkness nearly all day—only four hours of light in Fairbanks, Alaska, and absolutely *no* light in Inuvik, Canada!—and cities further south having still less-than-usual light—just nine hours in Washington, DC, and only eight hours in London. But cheer up—from here on out, the days will keep getting longer until June.

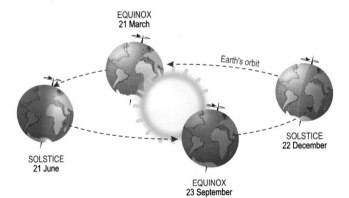

EQUINOX
21 March

Earth's orbit

SOLSTICE
22 December

SOLSTICE
21 June

EQUINOX
23 September

DEC 23

URSIDS METEOR SHOWER

The Ursids are a chilly affair but, with its occasional bursts of activity, one that keeps people watching. Lasting from December 17 through December 26, the peak usually occurs near the December solstice. At its peak, the shower can produce ten meteors per hour, but rare bursts can sometimes reach up to one hundred. For best viewing, bundle up and head outdoors in the early hours just before dawn on December 23. The source of the Ursids is the trail of comet 8P/Tuttle (and if you think you've kept hearing "Tuttle," that's because you have: H. P. Tuttle and his brother were both active astronomers after the Civil War and responsible for many discoveries).

METEOR SHOWER

RECURS ANNUALLY

CAN BE SEEN WITH NAKED EYE

BEST VIEWING TIME: just before dawn

PEAK: 10 meteors per hour

DIRECTION IN SKY: north (though meteors can radiate across most of the sky)

ABOUT BUSHEL & PECK BOOKS

Bushel & Peck Books is a children's publishing house with a special mission. Through our Book-for-Book Promise™, we donate one book to kids in need for every book we sell. Our beautiful books are given to kids through schools, libraries, local neighborhoods, shelters, nonprofits, and also to many selfless organizations that are working hard to make a difference. So thank you for purchasing this book! Because of you, another book will make its way into the hands of a child who needs it most.

NOMINATE A SCHOOL OR ORGANIZATION TO RECEIVE FREE BOOKS

Do you know a school, library, or organization that could use some free books for their kids? We'd love to help! Please fill out the nomination form on our website (see below), and we'll do everything we can to make something happen.

www.bushelandpeckbooks.com/pages/
nominate-a-school-or-organization

If you liked this book, please leave a review online at your favorite retailer. Honest reviews spread the word about Bushel & Peck—and help us make better books, too!